HEADWORK
ENGLISH
PROGRAMME 1

Chris Culshaw and Jill Dodgson

OXFORD UNIVERSITY PRESS

1994

Contents

Acknowledgements

The authors and publishers would like to thank the following for permission to reproduce copyright material:

John Adams Trading Company Ltd: 'Sunpower Kit', Catalogue 1992; **G. Barraclough Ltd**: 'Princes Jucee' packaging; **B.T. Batsford Ltd**: extract from Sheila Fergusson: *Growing Up in Victorian Times* (1977); **Cadbury Ltd**: 'Wispa' packaging; **Pie Corbett**: poem; **Early Learning Centre** and **Ritvik**: 'Megabloks' exclusive to Early Learning Centre, Catalogue 1992; **Faber and Faber Ltd**: extract from Betsy Byars: *The Midnight Fox* (1976); **Cassell plc**: extract from Nigel Rees: *Why Do We Say?* (Blandford Press, 1987); **Harvill** an imprint of **HarperCollins**: poem by Raymond Carver from *In A Marine Light* (Harvill 1987), Copyright © Raymond Carver 1984, 1985, 1986, 1987; **Hodder & Stoughton Ltd/New English Library**: extract from B.A. Phythian: *A Concise Dictionary of English Slang*, 3e (1986); **Lucasfilm Ltd**: transcript extract and stills from *Indiana Jones and The Temple of Doom*, TM & © Lucasfilm Ltd (LFL) 1984. All Rights Reserved; **Mars Confectionery**: 'Mars' bar packaging; **Nestle UK Ltd**: 'Smarties' packaging; **Newspaper Publishing plc**: 'Bestsellers at Hamleys' from *The Independent*; **Oxford University Press**: extract from Alan Spooner and John Weston: *Oxford Children's Dictionary*, extract from *The Oxford Children's Encyclopedia*, (1991), and extract from John Bailey (Ed): *Gods and Men*, (1981); **Pan Macmillan Children's Books**: extract from Peter Mayle: *Sweet Dreams and Monsters*, (Macmillan 1989); **Penguin Group Children's Publishing**: extract from Helen Morgan: *The Witch Doll*, copyright © Helen Morgan 1991, first published by Hamish Hamilton Ltd 1991; **Trebor Bassett Ltd**: 'Jelly Babies' packaging; **Vtech Electronics**: 'Talk-a-Lot' TM, Catalogue 1993; and **Walkers Smiths Snack foods Ltd**: 'Quavers' packaging. Also **Lowri Bond** and **Michael Hall** for their memories of toys, first published here, and the Area Organizer for Lancashire and Merseyside **Save The Children Fund**, for the quotation about Princess Anne.

The publishers would like to thank the following for permission to reproduce photographs:

John Adams p.48 (middle); **John Birdsall** p.49 (top); **Bill Bachman/Colorific** p.15; **Early Learning Centre** p.48 (right); **Mary Evans Picture Library** p.21 (top left); **Judy Harrison/Format** p.49 (bottom), **Maggie Murray/Format** p.49 (middle); **Kobal Collection** p.62 (top middle); **Lucas film Limited** pp.57, 58; **National Cycle Museum** p.21 (top right and middle left); **Peter Newark's Western Americana** pp.22, 27; **Raleigh Limited** p.21 (middle right); **1984 Tri-Star Pictures/Rex Features** p.62 (top left), **Rex Features** pp.62 (top right and bottom), 63; **V tech Electronics** p.48 (left); **John Walmsley** p.43.

Although every effort has been made to trace and contact copyright holders before publication this has not been possible in some cases. We apologise for any apparent infringement of copyright and will be pleased to rectify any errors or omissions at the earliest opportunity.

The illustrations are by **Juliet Breese** pp.36, 37, 38, 39, 44/5, 50, 51; **Chris Chaisty** pp.32, 47, 56, 61; **Tony Chance** pp.24, 25, 33, 46, 53; **Linda Jeffrey** pp.18, 19, 20, 60; **Pauline Little** pp.8/9; **Jill Newton** p.34, 54; **Rhiannon Powell** pp.28, 29, 30/1; **Judy Stevens** pp.21, 42, 49; **Jacqui Thomas** pp.6, 7; **Marc Vyvyan-Jones** pp.13, 14, 16, 40, 41, 52, 55.

Introduction

Dear Student

Welcome to the **Headwork English Programme**.

Each Students' Book is made up of nine short units. Every unit has a different theme, like holidays, games, food, or ambitions.

We have chosen stories, poems, scripts, photos, and pictures, as well as articles from newspapers and magazines, linked to these themes.

These are followed by **What to do** activities which will help you to develop a wide range of skills in speaking, reading, and writing.

At the start of each unit you will find a **Skills Panel**. This will tell you the main skills you will practise as you work through the unit.

At the end of each unit is a short **Review** which will help you to sum up your progress and talk about any questions you have on particular activities.

We hope you enjoy using **Headwork English Programme**.

Chris Culshaw and Jill Dodgson

Food Glorious Food

SKILLS YOU WILL USE IN THIS UNIT

1 Reading for enjoyment
2 Reading to find out information
3 Reading a poem
4 Thinking about advertising
5 Forming an opinion about what you read
6 Designing a poster and sweet packaging

A Meal to Remember

The only time I ever really enjoyed eating was one time over at Petie's house. Petie was a great eater, and he got an idea for a new food invention. It was called 'The Petie Burkiss Special'. He got his mum to make some dough, and then on top of this dough, Petie cut up dozens of hot sausages and luncheon meats and different kinds of cheese and pickles. Then he rolled it up and baked it, and when it came out of the oven it looked like a great golden football.

Petie sliced it right down the middle with a big knife and pushed half over to me. Wonderful-smelling steam poured up into my face. We started eating and our mouths were on fire and cheese and sausage juice was dripping down our chins. Petie was just moaning with happiness and I ate until my stomach hurt. It was the only time in my life that my stomach had hurt from being too full.

Betsy Byars (from *The Midnight Fox*)

What to do

On your own

1 Write down as many words as you can think of to describe the best eating experience you can imagine. Use the 5 headings given above, e.g. Sound, Taste, etc.

2 Choose one word from under each heading in your list and draw an illustration to go with each one.

3 Show your work to the group and tell them about the eating experience which would make you moan with happiness like Petie does in *A Meal to Remember*.

Grotty Borlotti

Mum went to a lecture and gave up meat.
Now she dishes up beans, 'just for a treat',
we get—

Creamy bran chunks or buckwheat bake,
brandied prune mousse and carrot cake.

Hazelnut tart with stir fried cheese,
garlic salad and herbal teas.

Mushroom pâté and split pea spread,
soya burger on curried bread.

Wholemeal pasta and a broadbean nutlet,
cashew nut soup and a chick pea cutlet.

Continental lentil or rice on toast,
grotty borlotti and dreaded nut roast.

Coconut chutney and beanshoot fritters,
It's boring beans that give us the jitters.

So, Dad and I took up jogging,
just down to the end of the street.
For it isn't too far
to the Hamburger Bar,
Where, 'just for a treat',
we'll stop—
and eat meat.

Pie Corbett

In pairs

1 Practise reading the poem aloud. Think about how the girl is feeling about her new diet as you read each verse.
2 Design a poster advertising the lecture Mum has been to. Include information which will persuade people to come. You will need to make up details about where and when the talk will take place, what it will be about, and about the speaker.
3 Role play a conversation between Mum and daughter on the subject of food. Imagine that Mum has found out about the trip to the Hamburger Bar.

Read the Label

What to do

In a small group

1 Decide whether these statements are true (T), false (F) or if there is is not enough evidence (NEE). Make a note of your answers.
   A Jucee is made by Smiths.
   B Both labels use illustrations to sell the product.
   C Drinking Jucee is better for you than eating Quavers.
   D Quavers are made in Reading, Berkshire.
   E Quavers give you more value for your money than Jucee.
   F The brand name of the drink is Quavers.
   G The seasonings used in Quavers are artificial.
   H E numbers 320 and 321 (in Quavers) are better for you than E numbers 221, 223, and 446 (in Jucee.)
   Compare your answers with other groups'.
2 List the words on the labels of Quavers or Jucee which might persuade shoppers to buy these products.

E numbers are labels given to food additives which the Common Market countries believe are safe to eat.

10

Sweet persuasion

1. **Mars** — INGREDIENTS: Sugar, Glucose Syrup, Skimmed Milk Powder, Hydrogenated Vegetable Fat, Cocoa Butter, Cocoa Mass, Whey Powder, Milk Fat, Milk Sugar, Fat reduced Cocoa Powder, Malt Extract, Emulsifier: Lecithin, Salt, Egg White, Hydrolysed Milk Protein, Flavouring. PLEASE DISPOSE OF THIS WRAPPER CAREFULLY - KEEP YOUR COUNTRY TIDY. A Mars a day helps you work, rest and play

2. **Bassetts Jelly Babies** — They're in a wibbly wobbly world of their own. e 113 g. STORE IN A COOL DRY PLACE. BEST BEFORE END-SEE TOP FLAP. TREBOR BASSETT LIMITED, MAIDSTONE ME16 0SP, ENGLAND. Ingredients: Sugar, Glucose Syrup, Water, Gelling Agent, Gelatin, Citric Acid, Flavourings. Colours: E104, E120, E132, E150. Please dispose of this wrapper carefully. "Keep your country tidy"

3. **Nestlé smarties** — ONLY SMARTIES HAVE THE ANSWER. Milk chocolate in a crisp sugar shell. INGREDIENTS: MILK CHOCOLATE, SUGAR, WHEAT FLOUR, EDIBLE STARCH, COLOURS (E171, E122, E110, E104, E101, E120, 132), FLAVOURING, GLAZING AGENT (CARNAUBA WAX).

4. **Cadbury's Wispa** — Textured Milk Chocolate Bar e 39 g. Ingredients: milk, sugar, cocoa butter, cocoa mass, vegetable fat, emulsifiers: 442 and soya lecithin, butterfat, flavourings. CADBURY QUALITY: We want you to enjoy this product. If you are not entirely satisfied with it, please return the complete package to our Consumer Services Manager, saying when and where purchased. If purchased in the Republic of Ireland, please return to Cadbury Ireland Ltd., Coolock, Dublin 5. CADBURY LIMITED, BOURNVILLE, BIRMINGHAM B30 2LU UK. Please dispose of this wrapper carefully "Keep your Country tidy"

What to do

In pairs

Make a note of which sweet packaging(s) (1-4):

A uses very bright colours
B has a rhyming slogan
C uses a pun or wordplay
D is aimed at young children
E is aimed at older children or adults
F shows that the sweets contain additives for colour
G shows some concern for the environment

What to do next

On your own

1 You have been asked by a well-known manufacturer to design packaging for a new sweet to appeal to young children. Make notes of your first ideas.
2 Draw your packaging and label the key features that will help to sell the product, e.g. catchy slogan, name in bold.

END OF UNIT REVIEW

1

2

TV

SKILLS YOU WILL USE IN THIS UNIT

1 Reading for meaning
2 Writing in clear sentences
3 Role playing a scene from a soap
4 Comparing your opinion with other people's
5 Conducting a survey of opinions and ideas
6 Writing a formal and an informal letter

Favourite Soaps

A

soap 1. Flattery. Usu. **soft soap**
2. [v.] Flatter. Ingratiate.
soap opera Radio or television
serial, often of trivial or sentimental
nature. Also **soap**.

Concise Dictionary of English Slang

B

soap A substance used
with water for washing.
soapy

Oxford Children's Dictionary

C **A Soap Opera**
This type of serial was first broadcast on radio, then on
TV, in the US. By the late 1930s they were being referred
to as 'soap operas' or 'soaps' or 'soapers' because the
original sponsors were soap manufacturers.

Nigel Rees (from *Why Do We Say?*)

What to do

In pairs

1 Why are certain TV programmes called 'soaps'?
2 Which of the definitions, A, B or C, helps you most to
answer question 1? Which helps you least?
3 Why might washing powder companies sponsor these
programmes?

In a small group

1 Each say which is your favourite 'soap'.
  What do you like about it?
2 Who is your favourite character in that soap?
  What kinds of thing does she/he do and say?
3 Who is your least favourite character?
  What does she/he do and say that makes you dislike her/him?

Help! Your favourite soap needs you!

You are sitting at home, watching your favourite soap. All of a sudden a large hand comes out of the screen and grabs you. A voice says, 'Quick, we need your help! Your favourite character is ill. You will have to step in and take their place.'

What to do

In a small group

1 Role play several scenes between each of your favourite characters and one or two other people also in the soap.
2 Rehearse each scene. Make an audio or videotape of the scene. Try to make your character speak and behave as they would in the 'soap'.

200 Channels!

In the future we may have as many as 200 TV channels to choose from.

What to do

In pairs

1 Do you think it will be good to have 200 TV channels? Give a reason for your answer.
2 Some new channels might show only one kind of programme, e.g. a horror film channel.
Do you think this would be a good idea? Give reasons for your answer.

What to do next

On your own

1 Carry out a survey in your group. Ask 6 to 8 people what kind of 'special' channel they would like to see on TV in the future and why. Record your findings in a chart like this:

Name	Special channel	Reason
Sita	Asian pop music	Because I like this music and other people might like it too if they heard it.

2 Use your chart to help you to write a letter to a broadcasting company. Tell them what kind of television programmes young people want in the future.

Japanese Pen-pal

You have a pen-pal in Japan. Her name is Yuko. She has asked you to videotape some English TV programmes for her to watch. She hopes the tape will help her to learn English. She would like a mixture of programmes: some for adults, some for children, some funny, and some serious. She also wants some information about each programme on the tape.

What to do

On your own

You will need a recent TV guide from a magazine or newspaper.

1 Make a list like this of 5 programmes that Yuko might find useful:

Name of programme	Channel	Day	Time	Length
Six O'clock News	BBC 1	Monday	6.00 pm	30 mins

2 You decide to send Yuko a 60 minute videotape. Decide on the extracts you will use from each programme and then list them like this:

> 10 minutes from 'Six O'clock News'
> 5 minutes from 'Cartoon Corner'

3 Write a letter to Yuko. Include 2 or 3 sentences about each extract so that she will know what kind of programme it is from and what age group it is for.

END OF UNIT REVIEW

1

2

Bike

SKILLS YOU WILL USE IN THIS UNIT

1 Making up a rhyming poem
2 Reading for information
3 Writing a story and an article
4 Drawing a simple sketch map
5 Designing a poster
6 Writing a dialogue with two points of view

Cycling Limericks

There was a young man called Lake
Who rode a bike with no brake.
He was ever so sorry
When he hit the lorry.
Please: don't make the same silly mistake.

There was an old man called Mike
Who borrowed his grandson's ....
He hit a cat in the .... ,
And ran over a toad.
Said Mike, 'I think it's safer to ....

There was a young woman called Sue Stile
Whose bike was too big, by a ....
She came to a sticky end
On a dangerous ....
We're still trying to fish her out of the Nile.

There was a young girl called ....
Who loved racing about at high ....
She dodged between ....
And jumped over prams.
A very reckless young cyclist indeed!

What to do

In pairs

1 Use these words to complete the 3 limericks.
   Or find other words that fit the blanks.
   - trike   - speed   - mile   - bend
   - road   - trams   - hike   - Reed
2 Each write out one of these limericks and illustrate it with
   your own cartoons.
3 Read the limericks aloud with your partner. Work out a way
   of sharing the reading. You could make an audio or video
   recording of your reading for the class.

What to do next

On your own

Make up 2 more cycling limericks and illustrate them. You
could choose a subject, such as cycle theft or cycle safety, and
use humour to give advice to young children.

church

START

main road

lift bikes over gate

farm track

muddy here

carry bikes across stream

up Beacon Hill — Steep

refreshments and first aid

along old railway — level but rough

FINISH

School

Three Borrowed Bikes

Three girls from the same school have borrowed bikes to take part in a bike race.

Karen

I've borrowed my brother's racing bike. It's light and fast, but it's a bit big for me. It's got narrow wheels and tyres, and 5 gears. I'm a bit scared about the race. I haven't been on a bike for years!

Liz

My sister lent me her new mountain bike. It's strong but very heavy. It's got 15 gears. The tyres are thick and wide, just right for rough riding. I'm not very fit or strong, so I've been doing some training!

Sharon

I've borrowed gran's old 'sit-up-and-beg' bike. The others think I'm mad! But I am the fittest girl in our year. I'm a good runner and swimmer and I'm in all the teams. The bike hasn't got any gears and it's a bit heavy. But I'm sure I'll win anyway.

On the left is the map of the race route.

18

In a small group

1 Decide which part(s) of the race Karen will find the hardest.
2 Where on the course do you think Liz might take the lead?
3 At what part of the race will Sharon's fitness help her?
4 Where in the race might accidents happen? Give reasons.
5 Which girl do you think will finish first?

What to do next

On your own

You go to the same school as Karen, Liz, and Sharon. You decide to enter the race. Just as the race is about to start, there is a terrible thunderstorm...

Write a story about the race. Use the map on page 18 to help you plan your story. You will need to invent details, such as times and dates, what kind of bike you are riding, etc. You can include your friends, teachers, and parents in your story, as well as the three girls.

Charity event

The teachers and pupils at your school want to organize a bike race for charity.

What to do

In a small group

1 Make a sketch map of the area around your school.
2 Draw the race route on your map.
   Mark any dangerous places where parents or teachers would have to stand in case of accidents. Mark where you would serve drinks.
3 Design a poster to advertise the race.
   This should include details, such as times, date, entry fee, age groups, prizes, etc.

Better by Bike?

A — Bikes are great. They keep you fit.

B — Bikes are hopeless in wet weather. You get cold and wet.

C — You can park a bike anywhere for free. But you have to pay for a car.

D — I have to dress smartly for work, so I can't turn up on a bike!

E — You can't carry things on a bike – like shopping.

F — Bikes are a very cheap way to get around.

G — Bikes are dangerous. You are much safer in a car.

H — Bikes are too slow. I'm always in a hurry.

I — They don't pollute the air. Bikes are good for the planet.

What to do

On your own

Use the opinions given above to make a table like this, showing the good and bad points of using a bike.

Advantages	Disadvantages
Cheap	Cold in winter

What to do next

On your own

Use the points in your table to help you write a conversation between a cyclist and a car driver about which is the best way to get around. It might start like this:

Cyclist: It's much cheaper to go by bike.
Driver: That's true, but you freeze on a bike in the winter!

Children's Bikes

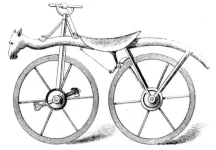

Hobby Horse bike, 1819

Velocipede, 1875

Tricycle, 1900

Mountain bike, 1993

What to do

In pairs

Use these photographs, the word bank, and the diagram below to help you to write a short article (10 to 12 sentences) called 'How Children's Bikes Have Improved in 200 Years'.

Word bank

light	plastic
heavy	rubber
speed	iron
steel	comfort
metal	safe
safety	wood
design	

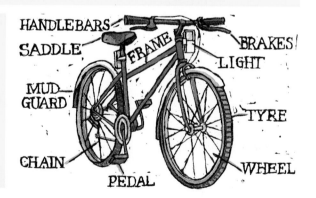

HANDLEBARS
SADDLE
FRAME
BRAKES
LIGHT
MUD GUARD
TYRE
CHAIN
PEDAL
WHEEL

END OF UNIT REVIEW

1

2

Outlaw

SKILLS YOU WILL USE IN THIS UNIT

1 Discussing facts and opinions
2 Reading a poem aloud
3 Thinking about the effects of language in poetry
4 Writing a newspaper report
5 Reading a poster for information

The Jesse James Story

During the Civil War between the Northern and Southern States of America, Jesse James and his brother Frank joined a band of soldiers and fought for the South. Jesse was only fourteen years old. The South lost the war and Jesse gave himself up to Northern soldiers. One story says Jesse was shot and badly wounded whilst under a white flag of truce. Jesse and Frank always claimed that they became outlaws because the Northerners were against them.

On 13 February 1866 Jesse and Frank robbed their first bank at a place called Liberty. They went from place to place robbing banks, trains, and sometimes small shops and rich individuals. If someone got in their way they were shot. Some people in the area did not mind the idea of banks being robbed because they belonged to the rich in the East. Other people in the cities of eastern America liked to hear such stories of daring deeds. The tales of Jesse and Frank spread far and wide. In 1881 the Governor of Minnesota offered a reward of $10,000 for the James brothers, dead or alive!

In 1882, whilst straightening a picture on the wall at home, Jesse was shot in the back of the head by one of his gang members – Robert Ford. Ford then claimed the reward. Frank gave himself up and went to court three times on murder and robbery charges. He was never found guilty.

What to do

In pairs

Discuss whether the following are true (T), false (F) or if there is not enough evidence (NEE). Make a note of your answers.
A Jesse learned a life of violence at an early age.
B Jesse became an outlaw because the Northerners were against him.
C Jesse robbed his first bank at a place called Freedom.
D Jesse only robbed from people who were very rich.
E Some people liked to hear stories of daring and violent deeds as long as they were not hurt themselves.
F Jesse was murdered by his brother Frank.
G Ford was more interested in money than friendship.

What to do next

On your own

You are writing the film script for *The Jesse James Story*. Choose one important moment in Jesse's life and write notes for that scene in the film. Use the headings in this example.

e.g. Moment when Jesse surrenders to Northern soldiers
  Setting: group of trees, barren land with boulders
  Characters: Jesse and Frank (aged 14–16), a band of soldiers
  Actions: Jesse and Frank crouched at edge of thicket, holding white flag, soldiers aiming rifles at them

The Ballad of Jesse James

1 Jesse James was a lad that killed many a man,
And robbed that Danville train,
But that dirty little coward that shot Mr Howard,
Has laid poor Jesse in his grave.
Chorus
>   Poor Jesse had a wife to mourn all her life,
>   His children they were brave,
>   Robert Ford caught his eye and shot him on the sly,
>   And they laid poor Jesse in his grave.

2 It was his brother Frank stuck up the Pittsfield Bank
And carried the money from the town,
It was in this very place that they had a little race,
For they shot Captain Sheets to the ground.
Chorus

3 They went to the crossing, not very far from there
And there they did the same
With the agent on his knees, he delivered up the keys,
To the outlaws, Frank and Jesse James.
Chorus

4 It was on a Wednesday night, the moon was shining bright,
    They stopped the Glendale train,
    He robbed from the rich and he gave to the poor,
    He'd a heart and a hand and a brain.
    Chorus

5 It was on a Saturday night, when Jesse was at home,
    Talking with his family brave,
    Robert Ford's pistol ball brought him tumblin' from the wall
    And then laid poor Jesse in his grave.
    Chorus

6 It was Robert Ford that dirty little coward,
    I wonder how he does feel,
    For he ate of Jesse's bread and he slept in Jesse's bed
    And then laid poor Jesse in his grave.
    Chorus

7 This song was made by Billy Gashade,
    As soon as the news did arrive.
    They said there was no man with the law in his hand,
    Could take Jesse James when alive.

    Anon

What to do

In a small group

1 Practise reading aloud *The Ballad of Jesse James.*
2 Look up the word **ballad** in a dictionary or an encyclopedia.
    How does the definition fit this poem?
    Give reasons for your answer.

Rhymes

In pairs

1   Match the words that rhyme in the list below,
    e.g. coward/Howard.

coward	grave	man	ball	Frank	same
train	made	Gashade	town	brave	bank
race	James	bright	bread	wife	place
sly	knees	bed	Howard	keys	brain
arrive	ground	life	night	wall	hand
alive	eye				

2   Say whether A or B best describes the rhyme pattern of the
    chorus on page 24:
    A The end of Line 2 rhymes with the end of Line 4. The
       middle words of Line 1 and Line 3 rhyme with the words
       at the end of these lines.
    B The end of Line 1 rhymes with the end of Line 3. The
       middle words of Line 2 and Line 4 rhyme with the words
       at the end of these lines.
    Compare your answers to questions 1 and 2 with another
    pair.

What to do next

On your own

1   Write a four-line chorus for a ballad about someone famous
    from the past or present. As the chorus will be repeated
    through the song, it should contain only important details
    about the person and their story. Use the same rhyme
    pattern as the chorus in *The Ballad of Jesse James*.
2   Some words in the ballad make the listener feel sorry for
    Jesse. Find any phrases like, 'His children they were brave'.
    Make a list of these.
3   How does the ballad describe Jesse's death? Which words
    make Jesse seem like a victim?
4   Write a newspaper report of Jesse James' death.
    Decide whether you will make Jesse sound like a victim or a
    villain. Try to choose a dramatic headline that shows this
    point of view like the ones below.

Villain shot at last!

Jesse betrayed!

Wanted

REWARD!
- DEAD OR ALIVE -

$5,000.00 will be paid for the capture of the men who robbed the bank at

NORTHFIELD, MINN.

They are believed to be Jesse James and his Band, or the Youngers.

All officers are warned to use precaution in making arrest. These are the most desperate men in America.

Take no chances! Shoot to kill!!

J. H. McDonald,
SHERIFF

What to do

In a small group

1 Who robbed the Northfield bank?
2 What are the dangers of the instructions in the last line of this poster?
3 In America it is still easy and common for people to own guns. List the arguments a police officer might use against making gun ownership easy in Britain.

END OF UNIT REVIEW

1
2

Unit 5

Animal Lessons

SKILLS YOU WILL USE IN THIS UNIT

1 Finding out about fables, myths, and legends
2 Reading fables and myths for enjoyment
3 Understanding character and plot
4 Planning, telling, and writing stories

Aesop's Fables

A **fable** is a short story that teaches a lesson. Many fables have animals as their characters, who act and speak like humans.

Read the following fables which were probably first written down about 3,000 years ago by a Greek slave called Aesop.

The hare and the tortoise

One day a tortoise and a boastful hare argued about which of them was faster. They agreed to settle the matter by running a race. The hare sprinted away leaving the tortoise far behind. She thought that she would win easily and so halfway round decided to lie down and have a sleep. The tortoise knew that he was really much slower than the hare but kept plodding away steadily. The tortoise overtook the sleeping hare, kept going, and went on to win the race – and the argument.

Digging for treasure

A dying farmer wanted his children to become good farmers when he had gone. He told them, 'Go and dig in my potato field. You will find there the treasure I have to leave you.'

The three children dug and dug but could find nothing. They were very disappointed because there was no gold or jewels.

Later that year the field gave a giant crop of potatoes because it had been so well dug over.

The snake and wasp

A wasp landed on a snake's head and started stinging. It would not let go. The snake was mad with pain and anger. It couldn't think of how to get its own back on the wasp.

Finally the snake slid its head under the wheel of a passing cart. Both the wasp and the snake died together.

What to do

In a small group

1 Choose one lesson or moral from the ones given below to fit these stories. Make sure that you all agree on your group decision.
   The hare and the tortoise
   • Do not fall asleep in the middle of a race.
   • If you are over confident in your ability you may fail.
   • Keep trying and you will succeed in the end.
   Digging for treasure
   • Do not expect something for nothing.
   • Learn to value what your parents give you.
   • Hard work has its own rewards.
2 Discuss what you think *The snake and the wasp* says about human behaviour. Agree on one sentence that sums up the moral of the story.

Neighbours

A fox and an eagle became friends. They decided to live near each other so that they could see more of one another. The eagle built a nest at the top of a tall tree and laid four shining eggs. The fox made a den in some bushes at the bottom of the tree and soon gave birth to four lovely cubs.

One sunny day the fox went hunting for food to feed her family. The eagle happened to be feeling very hungry so she swooped down and picked up the cubs one at a time. She took each one to her nest and shared them with her eaglets. When the fox came back she was very angry because the eagle had eaten her cubs. The fox forgot her motherly feelings. She just wanted to get her own back on the bird. The eagle had a great advantage because she could fly. How could the fox get back at her one-time friend?

A few days later the fox had her opportunity. When the eagle was out flying, she spotted some people cooking a rabbit on a campfire. She swooped down and picked up some bits of meat which they had thrown in the ashes. She returned to the nest delighted with her find. Just as the eagle dropped the charred meat into the nest a wind sprang up.

The wind fanned the smouldering meat which set fire to the dry twigs of the nest. As the nest burned the young eagles dropped to the ground. The fox seized her opportunity and gobbled up every one of the young in front of their mother's eyes.

What to do

In pairs

1 Each make sketches to show what happens in paragraphs 1-4 of *Neighbours*. Give each of the 4 drawings a heading,

e.g. 1 *The fox and eagle friends build their homes.*

2 With your partner, choose 3 adjectives from this list which describe the eagle's character and 3 words which describe the fox's:

greedy motherly selfish
vengeful stupid careless
friendly wicked

3 Decide which of the following adjectives best describes the fox's feelings when she discovers the theft of her cubs:

upset angry helpless
sorrowful vengeful lonely
indifferent

Think of 2 adjectives which might describe how the fox feels when she sees the young birds falling from their nest. The illustrations should help you.

4 Which of these is the most important lesson to be learnt from this fable?

- Do not enter into friendships lightly.
- Do not betray the trust of your friends.
- One bad turn deserves another.
- Greed will get the better of you.

What to do next

On your own

Rewrite this fable to give younger children a positive lesson about friendship. Change the story so that the fox saves the young eagles as they fall from the nest. Give the fox's reasons for doing this and say how the eagle reacts.

Telling Stories

Fables come from a time when most people did not read or write. These stories were handed down 'by word of mouth'. As people told and retold fables they often added details or changed them a little but the moral usually stayed the same.

A The travellers and the bear   **B** The lion and the mouse   **C** The dog and the bones

What to do

In a small group

1 Look at pictures A, B, and C which each sum up a story with a moral. Each pick a different story and decide on 3 main events to fit the picture and its moral.
e.g. *The travellers and the bear*
　　1　Two friends go for a walk together.
　　2　They are attacked by a bear.
　　3　One character climbs a tree leaving her friend to save herself.

2 Each take a turn to tell your story to the group, using your ideas from question 1. Improve the stories as you tell them with as many extra details as you can.

3 When you feel confident, share your stories with your class. Listen to how other groups tell your chosen story. List any details they include which help make it interesting.

Legends and Myths

Many kinds of stories were passed on from one person to another in ancient times. **Legends** were made as news of heroic deeds travelled from place to place. People made **myths** to reassure themselves about why certain frightening or amazing things happened.

Legends

Legends are stories about real people who are famous for doing something brave or extraordinary. Usually there is a germ of truth, but the original story may have been exaggerated as people have told and retold it.

Myths

Long ago our ancestors were frightened by things like thunder and lightning; maybe they thought it was the Sky Gods getting angry? Myths are tales like this which helped to explain events, such as thunderstorms, why night followed day or even how men and women were first created.

Adapted from
Oxford Children's Encyclopedia

What to do

On your own

Write down the missing words in the correct order from 1–8.
    moral   legends   tales   television
    people   fables   behaviour   myth

Our ancestors passed down many ....1....... from one generation to another. Stories such as myths, ...2........ and ....3........ were an early way of getting information and being entertained like ....4....... is today. A fable is a story that often has a ....5........ . It teaches a lesson about people's ......6....... . A ....7....... is a story which tries to explain the natural world. A legend is often about ....8....... who do great deeds or make dangerous journeys.

The fire children

One day two spirit people who lived inside the Sky God, Nyame, climbed up to his mouth to look out. He sneezed and they fell down to the earth he had made. They had to make a new home because they couldn't get back.

The female spirit, Iyaloda, began to get lonely while the man spirit was out all day. Her loneliness made her grumpy and sad until she thought of a plan. The plan seemed so simple that the man spirit agreed to what she said.

'If we take some clay and mould some small creatures shaped like ourselves, we can bake them in the fire and then breathe life into them so that they move about like us. Then they'll be able to keep me company and I won't be lonely. We could call them children.'

The two spirits modelled the little figures and put them in the fire to bake. Just at that moment they heard the Sky God, Nyame, coming. They pulled the clay figures out of the fire and hid them in case they got told off for making them. Nyame often dropped in to visit them during his stay on earth. Each time that he came, they either hid the figures or left them baking until he had gone.

At last Nyame went back to the sky and the spirit people took out all the children and looked at them. Some were hardly baked at all. They were quite white. Others had turned yellow; some were baked red or brown; some were burned quite black.

The spirit people were delighted with all the children they had made, whatever the colour. They breathed their breath into each of them, so they came to life, just like children waking up from sleep.

Iyaloda, the Great Mother, was lonely no longer.

John Bailey (adapted from Gods and Men)

What to do

On your own

1 Put the things that the spirit people do in order:
   A Talk to a god.
   B Breathe life into children.
   C Fall from the sky.
   D Bake clay models.
   E Talk about a plan.
   F Live in a new home.

2 Give one adjective to describe Iyaloda's feelings as she does each of these things.
   e.g. *C Fall from the sky = afraid or shocked*

3 Complete these sentences.
   The characters are different from characters in modern stories because...
   The characters are similar to characters in modern stories because...

4 Imagine the setting where this myth takes place. We do not learn much about this from the story itself.
   Give details of the place where the spirit people live and the area around them.

5 Write 2 to 3 sentences that explain why this story is a myth. Think about where it comes from and what the story is about. If you need to remind yourself of the definition of a myth look at page 33.

END OF UNIT REVIEW

1
2

35

Wordplay

SKILLS YOU WILL USE IN THIS UNIT

1 Thinking about spelling patterns
2 Using a dictionary
3 Thinking up jokes
4 Thinking about words with more than one meaning
5 Making up definitions

Missing Letters

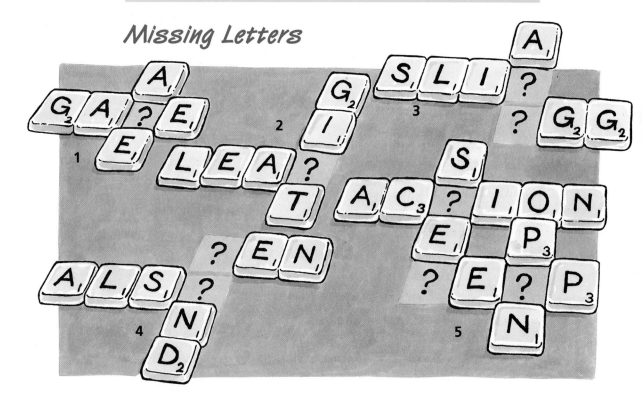

What to do

On your own

What letters would fit into the spaces in puzzles 1–5?
Write your answers like this:

What to do

On your own

1 How many words with 4 letters can you make by putting letters from the stand into the space?

2 How many words with 5 letters can you make here?

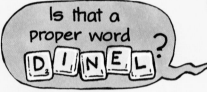

Is that a proper word DINEL?

If you are not sure you have made a proper word, check using a dictionary.

What to do next

In a small group

1 How many words can you make from these 7 letters?

Set out your answers like this:

2 letter	3 letter	4 letter	5 letter
an	ant	pant	

2 If you could pick any 7 Scrabble tiles, which would you pick to make the most words?
Use Scrabble tiles (or small cards with letters on) and see if you can find the best selection of letters.
It may help if you each work with different sets of letters and then decide on the best set.
Write 3 or 4 sentences about what your group discovers.
You might start like this:

To make a lot of words you need…

A Sign of the Times

What to do

On your own

Which word in each of these signs makes them funny?

What to do next

In pairs

Match shops 1-6 with signs A-F. Write your answers like this:

Sign A goes with Shop…

Shops

Signs

A Out to lunch, give me a ring.

B Back in A flash

C Out, but wheel be back soon. X

D Just nipped out for a bite.

E Having a long break

F GONE TO MEAT A FRIEND

39

One Letter Wrong

A I'm your Hairy Godmother.

B Rover is our new guard hog.

C The police caught the rubbers in the bank.

D We are moving into a new mouse next week.

E The fairy gave Sarah three washes.

What to do

On your own

1 Write each sentence as it should be.

2 Pick one of the 'wrong' sentences and draw a cartoon to go with it.

3 Make up some more 'one letter wrong' sentences.
Draw some cartoons to illustrate them.

Backwords

If you eat bacon backwards, you get a 'nocab'.
A nocab is a bad pain in the neck.
If you swim backwards, you get 'miws'.
Miws are bubbles up your nose.

What to do

On your own

1 Complete these backword definitions:

> If you play a flute backwards you get an 'etulf'.
> An etulf is...
> If you ride a bike backwards you get an...
> An... is...

2 Make up 6 to 8 more backwords. Set them out like this.

Word	Backword	Meaning
skate	etaks	small bugs that live in your socks
video	oediv	

3 Illustrate some of your backwords with cartoons.

END OF UNIT REVIEW

1

2

Toys

SKILLS YOU WILL USE IN THIS UNIT

1 Discussing your opinion with others
2 Reading and writing autobiography
3 Reading for information
4 Making a storyboard
5 Writing and drawing to give information

What Do You Think?

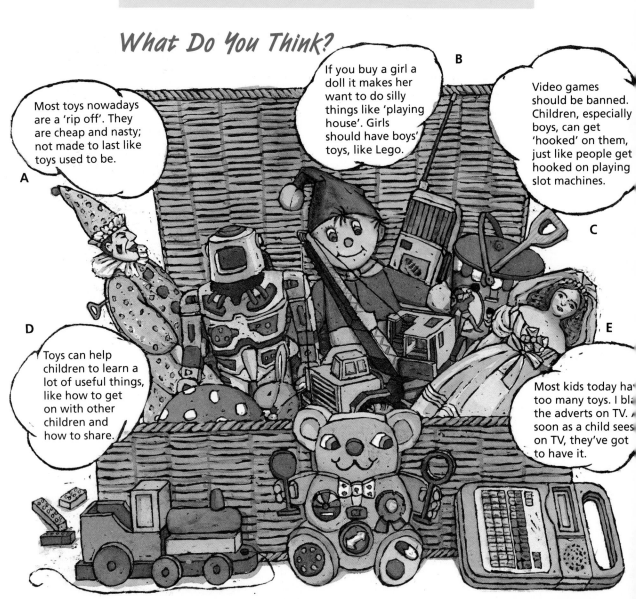

What to do

In a small group

1 Say if you agree or disagree with each of the statements
   A-E on page 42. Give reasons for your opinions.
2 Find someone in your group who disagrees with you on any
   of the statements on page 42.
3 Write 2 or 3 sentences about how your views differ.
   Set them out like this:

   > I disagree with Tamsin about statement B
   > Tamsin thinks that… But I think that…

Memories of Toys

My favourite toy was a large giraffe. I got it when
I was six. It's hard to say why it's so special. Maybe
it's because it's unusual, not like a teddy or a doll.
It seemed very big when I was little. I remember
once, it got really mucky because I used to drag it
all round the streets. Mum said it had to be washed
so I hid it. But she found it and put it in the washing
machine. I cried when I saw it going round and round.
I shouted, 'You've drownded Jaffa!' I take it everywhere. It's going to university with me next year.

Lowri (age 17)

My best ever toy was Workshop Willy. It's a type of little
man. You took it to bits then made it again, with nuts
and bolts. It was like a robot figure. You hammered his
hat on. I liked it because my dad's a builder and mum
gave it me when I was born. I've had it all my life, I
suppose.

Michael (age 10)

What to do

On your own

1 Write 3 or 4 sentences about your own favourite childhood
   toy and the memories you have of it.
2 Ask the members of your group what their favourite toys
   are. Make a list of these and compare it with the best-
   selling toys listed on page 44.

43

Best Sellers

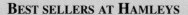

These were the best-selling toys at a big London toyshop for Christmas 1992.

BEST SELLERS AT HAMLEYS

1 Sega Video Games System, Mega Drive, £129.99.
2 Nintendo Video Games Systems, Super NES, £129.99.
3 Tomy Char-G's. Remote control that wheels and spins, £17.99.
4 Trolls from 99p to £49.99.
5 Lego Pirate Island, £24.99.
6 Tobias, Hamleys 1992 limited edition Steif bear, £99.99.
7 Atmosfear, an interactive board/video game by Spears, £24.99.
8 Barbie Magic House, portable doll's house, £39.99.
9 Changeable pens. Felt tip pens that change colour, £3.99.
10 Blitzer, hand-held airbrush using felt-tip pens, £7.99.

Thunderbirds does not appear because of lack of availability.

The Independent 17 December 1992

What to do

In a small group

1 Look at each toy in the list above and say why you think it is popular. Decide which age group it is best for. Is it more suitable for a girl or a boy?

2 Which new toys or games do you think will be on this year's best seller list?

A hundred and fifty years ago

Toys, hobbies, and games

Many toys given to Victorian children were beautifully made by craftsmen and some have survived until today. Carved wooden farm animals or a Noah's ark, dolls' houses with accurate miniature furniture, beautifully dressed wax or china dolls, wooden Dutch dolls, rag dolls, hobby horses, toy soldiers, musical boxes, peep-shows, and toy theatres were popular well-made toys. Constructional and educational toys, such as sets of building materials, alphabet

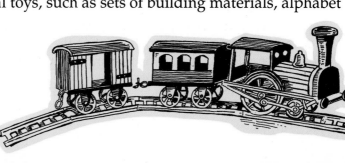

bricks and clock-work models of steam ships or railway locomotives, began to appear. Hobbies involving collections were encouraged by parents as educational pursuits – birds' eggs, butterflies, pressed wild flowers, shells, and (after 1840) stamps.

Sheila Fergusson (from *Growing Up in Victorian Times*)

What to do

In a small group

Make a list of all the toys mentioned in the extract and say if children still play with this kind of toy today. Set your list out like this:

Toy	Still popular today	Not used nowadays
Wooden farm animals	✓	

What to do next

In pairs

1 You have each been asked to choose one modern toy to go into a local toy museum.
These toys will be put on display, so that children coming to the museum in 100 years' time can see and read about them.
Which toy would you pick and why? Discuss your choice with your partner.

2 Each toy in the museum has a label giving information about it.
Write a label for your chosen toy. Make sure that the label includes the date the toy was made, its price, the age group it was used by, and the name of the person (you) who donated it. Then write 2 or 3 sentences about why the toy was popular and fun to play with.

3 Swap labels with your partner and imagine you are a child visiting the museum in 100 years' time. Write your reaction to the information on the label and to the toy itself.
Remember, as a child living in the year 2100 you will think today's toys are very strange.

The Witch Doll

Linda has been given an old doll by Mr Baldock, a rag and bone man. The doll is inside a bag. Linda is outside her front door with the bag when Joanna, a girl who lives nearby, comes over to her.

'Is this it?' asked Joanna, looking with disgust at the grubby old workbag, with its cross-stitch embroidery. 'What's in it?' She pulled the wooden handles apart and peered into the bag. 'A doll!' she said, scornfully. 'Don't tell me you still play with dolls?'

'Not really,' Linda lied. 'I was only going to change...' Joanna had thrust her hand into the bag and grasped the little wooden doll round its middle. She pulled it out into the sunlight, saying, 'It's hideous. I'm not surprised old Baldy gave it to you. I never saw such an ugly face.'

With the sickening click of a mousetrap, the upraised arms of the doll came down and snapped themselves tightly across the back of Joanna's hand.

Joanna dropped the workbag and screamed – but no sound came from her. Petrified, Linda sat staring at her. Her face was distorted with pain, her eyes wild and wide, her mouth held open in a silent scream.

Suddenly coming to life, Linda sprang to her feet and snatched at the doll, pulling at its arms, trying to prise them from Joanna's hand, not caring if she broke the beastly thing.

Under Linda's eager fingers the doll's arms rose smoothly and easily, leaving two deep red marks on the back of Joanna's hand.

'You might have warned me,' Joanna said, putting her hand to her mouth and sucking at it.

'I didn't know it was going to do that.' Linda stooped to pick up the workbag. 'I've only just had the thing.'

She looked at the doll she was holding. It was just an ordinary wooden doll, a little old-fashioned looking, perhaps, but pretty much like any other wooden doll; stiff legs, stiff arms, stiff body, egg-shaped head. It was difficult to believe there could possibly be anything odd about it.

Joanna was looking at it too, still sucking the back of her bruised hand.

46

'That's funny,' she said. 'Its face looks quite different now. It looked hideously cross before.'

'How could it?' Linda asked. There was a queer, tight feeling in her stomach. 'It's only a doll. Dolls can't change their expressions.'

But she knew this one could.

Helen Morgan

What to do

In pairs

1 Do you think Linda and Joanna are friends? Give reasons.
2 Why do you think the doll trapped Joanna's hand?
3 Why did Linda not warn Joanna about the doll?
4 How did Joanna feel about the doll?
5 Did Linda feel the same?
6 Use a dictionary to check the meanings of these words:
   - scornfully   - hideous   - petrified   - distorted

What to do next

On your own

You work for a film studio that wants to make a cartoon about *The Witch Doll*. Before you make the cartoon you need to sketch out a storyboard. This is what the storyboard might look like for the start of the film:

Think about what might happen next and set it out like this storyboard with some simple sketches and captions.

Teaching Toys

Some toys are sold as 'educational' toys. Their makers advertise these as toys that help children to learn and play. Here are three examples of educational toys.

TALK-A-LOT

Ages 2½ and up

- Four play modes include telephone, numbers, colours, & music learning play. 'Speed dial' numbers call ten characters & phrases.
- Call the clown, teacher, baker, video store helper, & more!
- Characters actually 'call' the child back.
- Four sound effects add to the fun.
- Phone stand holds phone when not in use.
- Volume control switch built-in.
- Battery operated (4 LR6 batteries not included).

£17.99 approx.

610 Sunpower Kits

A fascinating introduction to solar power. 2 card models (windmill and carousel) to colour, cut out and assemble and power with a motor and solar cell (hence no batteries needed!). Even the felt pen is included. Will work under a spotlight or in direct sunlight. Ages 8 - 12

£9.95

MEGABLOCKS 90 PIECES

£9.99

Create endless different structures with this super value container of building blocks. 90 brightly coloured pieces compatible with the leading brand.
Age 1½ - 5. **Ref 1643**

What to do

On your own

Write a sentence like this for each of the 3 toys above:

Megabloks: This toy will help children to learn about...

What to do next

On your own

Choose 3 more toys from the list below. Write a similar sentence about each toy to persuade an adult that it is a good toy to buy for a young child.

- chess set
- kite
- bucket and spade
- cricket set
- tricycle
- doll
- set of felt pens
- plasticine

Special Children... Special Toys

Euan
(aged 4)
is blind

David
(aged 6)
is deaf

Simi
(aged 9) is
physically
handi-
capped

1. ROLLER SKATES
2. FOOTBALL
3. WATER PISTOL
4. PAINTBOX
5. SLIDE
6. RADIO CONTROLLED CAR
7. LEGO
8. BOXING GLOVES
9. SWING
10. VIDEO GAME
11. BARBIE DOLL

What to do

In a small group

Make 2 lists for each of the children using headings like:
'Toys that Euan could play with' and 'Toys that could be
modified for Euan'.

What to do next

On your own

Pick one of the toys above and write 2 or 3 sentences to say
how it could be modified for one (or more) of the 3 children.
You could also include some simple drawings.

END OF UNIT REVIEW

1
2

Sleep and Dreams

SKILLS YOU WILL USE IN THIS UNIT

1 Drawing and labelling diagrams
2 Writing a letter
3 Reading for meaning
4 Reading and writing a poem
5 Comparing your ideas with other people's
6 Writing a clearly structured story

Million Dollar Bed

Ben is motor-bike mad. He has decided to enter this competition. This is his design for his 'dream bed'.

DESIGN YOUR DREAM BIKER'S BUNK
Win a day out at Donnington, at the British Motorcycle Grand Prix.

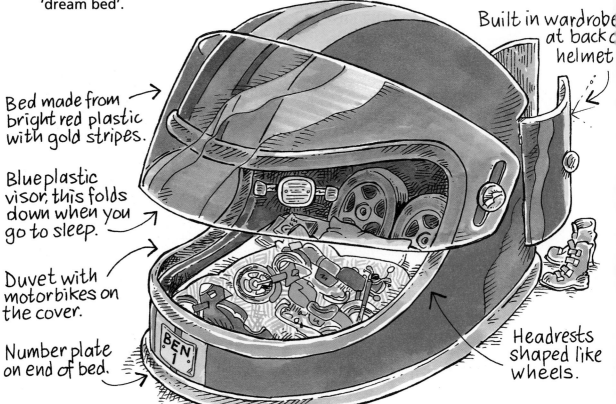

Bed made from bright red plastic with gold stripes.

Blue plastic visor, this folds down when you go to sleep.

Duvet with motorbikes on the cover.

Number plate on end of bed.

BEN 1

Built in wardrobe at back of helmet

Headrests shaped like wheels.

On your own

1 Make a chart like this one to show what you think are the good and bad points of Ben's design.

Good points	Bad points
It is very colourful	Could be dangerous in a fire

2 Use your chart to complete this sentence:

I think Ben's design would/would not win a prize because…

On your own

1 Design your own 'dream' bed or bedroom.
Be creative. Anything is possible.
Draw your bed/bedroom. Label it clearly to show what materials and colours you would use.
2 Complete these sentences about your design.

The most unusual thing about my bed/bedroom is…
I think my friends would like my bed/bedroom because…
If I had a sign on my bed/bedroom door it would say…
My bed/bedroom tells you something about my personality because…

3 Find out the names and addresses of some companies that make beds. You might get this information from the 'Yellow Pages' or from local furniture stores.
Write to one of these companies. Ask them to send you a catalogue showing the beds they make. Do they make any unusual beds?

Sleep and Dreams: the Facts

Believe it or not… we spend about one third of our lives asleep. By the time we are 60 years old we will have slept for 20 years! Nobody knows why we sleep or why we dream.

When we dream our eyes flicker. These movements are called REMs – 'rapid eye movements'.

Most people dream for about 2 hours each night. Dreams usually last for 5 or 10 minutes. But they can go on for 2 hours.

Some people say they never dream. They probably do have dreams, but never remember them.

We move about a lot when we are asleep. The average person changes position 40 times during the night. Girls sleep more deeply than boys.

Most people talk in their sleep and some people walk in their sleep! About 1 in 5 children sleep-walk.

What to do

In pairs

Say whether these statements are true (T), false (F) or if there is not enough evidence (NEE).
A Most adults have nightmares.
B Some people sleep-walk and dream at the same time.
C Dreams can last up to 2 hours.
D Birds sleep, but fish do not.
E We sleep because we have to rest our brains.
F We dream between 5 and 10 dreams every night.
G Most young people sleep-walk.
H Men talk in their sleep more than women.
I Some people cannot remember having any dreams.

Sleeping

He slept on his hands.
On a rock.
On his feet.
On someone else's feet.
He slept on buses, trains, in airplanes.
Slept on duty.
Slept beside the road.
Slept on a sack of apples.
He slept in a pay toilet.
In a hayloft.
In the Super Dome.
Slept in a Jaguar, and in the back of a pickup.
Slept in theatres.
In jail.
On boats.
He slept in line shacks and, once, in a castle.
Slept in the rain.
In blistering sun he slept.
On horseback.
He slept in chairs, churches, in fancy hotels.
He slept under strange roofs all his life.
Now he sleeps under the earth.
Sleeps on and on.
Like an old king.

Raymond Carver

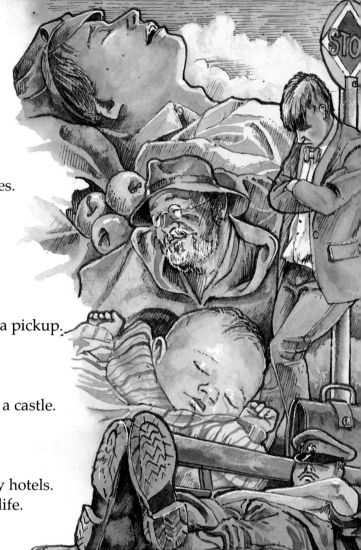

What to do

In a small group

Look at each occasion when the man slept and try to work out
where he was and why he slept there.

e.g. 'He slept on his hands.' This might be talking about him
falling asleep at his desk at school.

What to do next

On your own

Write a 'sleeping' poem about your own life. Set it out like
Raymond Carver's.

Sweet Dreams?

A dictionary of dreams

A **Ant**: If you dream of ants, you should expect many little worries during the day.

Apples: This is a good dream for most people, but if you dream of apples on the ground this means you have a false friend.

B **Badger**: This is a sign of good luck.

Beans: This is a bad dream. To dream of beans growing means sickness for your children.

C **Cheese**: To dream of cheese means you will soon be disappointed.

Clock: To see or hear a clock means danger from an enemy.

Gustav Miller

Dreams that come true

Once upon a time there was a very old man who had a dream about a big tiger. In his dream, the tiger followed him home from the supermarket. The old man was very scared, so he locked his door and went to bed. But then the tiger jumped in through the window, and he came up to the old man and he bit him hard on the toe. He bit him so hard that the old man woke up. And do you know what happened? He really had been bitten on the toe – by his false teeth. They had dropped out while he was sleeping.

And then there was a little girl who dreamed that she had a hairy chest that was making funny noises every time she touched it. And when she woke up, she found her cat fast asleep on her chest and purring.

There are hundreds of different dreams like this, started off by something you can feel or hear in your sleep – a thunderstorm, the telephone ringing in another room, the sound of an aeroplane flying over the house, the blankets falling off the bed and making you dream you're at the coldest part of the North Pole. What makes them different from other dreams is that your brain picks up something that is really happening and makes it part of a dream.

Peter Mayle

What to do

In a small group

When you have read these extracts discuss these questions.
1 Do you believe that some dreams are caused by things we feel or hear in our sleep? What other things might cause this kind of dream?
2 Do you think your dreams have meanings – like the meanings from 'A dictionary of dreams'?
3 Do you ever have bad dreams? If so, what do you think causes them?

What to do next

On your own

Write a story or a poem called 'The Dream Machine'. Describe the machine – its size, colour, shape, and the noise it makes. Say who made it and why. Explain what it does.
    You have been asked to test it. How do you feel before you use it? What happens when you test it?

END OF UNIT REVIEW

1
2

Heroes and Heroines

SKILLS YOU WILL USE IN THIS UNIT

1 Reading a scene from a film-script
2 Thinking about characters, plot, and location
3 Improvising a scene for a film
4 Writing a scene from a film-script
5 Writing to give your opinion

Into the Temple of Doom

Read the following extract from the film, *Indiana Jones and the Temple of Doom,* in groups of 3.

Indiana Jones is a university professor who has a habit of getting into amazing adventures.

Short Round is a Japanese boy who is Indiana Jones' friend and assistant.

Willy is a cabaret singer who is accidentally caught up in Indiana's adventure.

Indiana Jones and his young friend Short Round are at the start of a hidden passage. The passage leads from Willy's room to the secret Temple of Doom.

Indiana Jones: Stay behind me, Short Round. Step where I step and don't touch anything.

Short Round: (*Knocks switch on wall... two mummies burst out!*) Oooh! I step where you step. I touch nothing!

Willy: (*From outside*) Indy!

Short Round: I step on something?

Indiana Jones: Yes, there's something on the ground.

Short Round: Feel I step on fortune cookies.

Indiana Jones: It's not fortune cookies. Let me take a look.

(*Lights match and masses of insects are seen crawling everywhere.*)

Short Round: (*Large praying mantis on arm*) That's no cookie!

Indiana Jones: It's alright. I got it. (*Picks it off*) Ouch! Now go, there go. (*Points to a clear corridor in distance*)

(*Both continue stepping carefully. Short Round treads on a false paving stone and a millstone rolls over the exit behind them. The way on is also blocked. They are trapped in a small chamber. Indiana lights a rag torn from a skeleton. Short Round moves towards him.*)

Indiana Jones: Stop! Look, just stand up against the wall, will you?

(*Short Round, hands in pockets, leans against the wall and presses another stone lever. Rollers creak and the roof begins to lower.*)

Short Round: You say to stand against the wall. Stand against the wall you say. It's not my fault!

Indiana Jones: Willy, get in here! Willy!! Willy!!

Willy: (*In bedroom and complaining*) Here I get all dirty again.

Short Round: It's not my fault.

Indiana Jones: We're in trouble!

Willy: Trouble. Trouble? What sort of trouble? (*Pushes statue and enters the tunnel to see the two mummies*) AAaagh!

(*The roof, in the chamber where Indiana and Short Round are, gets lower, long spear-like spikes come out from floor and ceiling. Skeletons, skulls and debris rise as if alive.*)

Indiana Jones: This is serious!

Willy: (*Shrieking*) There are two dead people down here!

Indiana Jones: There's gonna be two dead people in here. Hurry!

Willy: I've almost had enough of you two.

Indiana Jones: Willy!

Willy: What's the rush!

Indiana Jones: It's a long story, Willy. Hurry or you don't get to hear it!

Willy: (*In the dark walking over the insects*) Ohh God! What is this? Indy, what is this? I can't see a thing.

Indiana Jones: Hurry!

Willy: Alright! (*Almost crying*) Oh, I broke a nail. (*Seeing insect on her hand – then insects all around*) Oooh, Oogh. Aarghh!

Short Round: Willy, hurry!!

Willy: They're in my hair!

Indiana Jones: Oh shut up, Willy!

Willy: Indy, let me in!

Short Round: Let us out!

Willy: Let me in!!

Short Round: Let us out!!

Indiana Jones: Listen! Shut up!!

Willy: (*Pleading*) Let me in. They're all over my hair!

Indiana Jones: There's got to be a fulcrum release lever here somewhere!

Willy: A what!

Indiana Jones: A handle that opens the door.

Willy: There are, there are two square holes!

Indiana Jones: Go to the right hole!

Short Round: Hurry, lady.

Willy: (*Gingerly putting hand in hole*) Ooooh. AArrrgggg!!

   (*Screams as Indiana Jones' hand grabs hers*)

Indiana Jones: The other one! The other right! Your other right! The one on your right!!

Willy: I'm sorry. I'm sorry – I can't do it!

Indiana Jones: You can do it. Feel inside!

Willy: (*Angrily, seeing the hole full of insects*) You feel inside!!

Indiana Jones: Do it NOW!

Willy: OK! (*Starts whimpering*) Ooooh!

Indiana Jones: (*Slowly and surely*) Willy, we are gonna die!!

Willy: It's moving!... Got it!!

   (*Triumphant music. Stones roll back, ceiling rises, spikes retract. Willy enters shrieking.*)

Willy: Get them off of me. Get them off of me. They're all over me. Get them off of me!!

   (*Willy pushes the lever with her bottom as she bends over to scratch. Ceiling descends. Spikes rise. Stones start rolling.*)

Short Round: It wasn't me! It's her! Come on! Come on!

Indiana Jones: (*Grabs Willy and pushes her out of the closing doorway*) Come on! Move!!

   (*Stones meet behind them but not before Indiana Jones has snatched his fallen hat from the chamber floor.*)

What to do

In a small group

1 Make a diagram of the tunnel where the action takes place. Label the things which surprise the characters.
2 Explain how the trap, which they get caught in, works.
3 Imagine you are the musical director and decide what kind of music should be played when:
   • Indiana Jones and Short Round find the two mummies
   • the spikes come down in 'the chamber of death'
   • Willy pulls the lever and saves the situation

On your own

1 Using your dictionary, check any meanings of these adjectives which you are unsure of.

- clever
- bossy
- young
- careless

- funny
- brave
- weak
- boring

- selfish
- vain
- loyal
- resourceful

- helpful
- caring
- strong
- complaining

2 Write down 4 or 5 of these words which describe Willy.
3 Write down 4 or 5 of them that describe Indiana Jones.
4 Describe each of these characters in one clear statement.

Plotting the action

What to do

In a small group

1 Read the outlines on page 61 for plot A and plot B for two new Indiana Jones adventures.
2 Discuss in detail what might happen in each story.
3 Choose one plot and divide the events into 2 or 3 scenes. Write notes under Scene headings to show the action that will take place, like this:

Scene 1: Indiana Jones and his friends visit the Prime Minister.
He asks them to help with the mystery of the Underground tube train station. People keep going missing in the same station.

4 Improvise your Indiana Jones adventure, using the scene notes you have already made. Your adventure should last about 5 minutes.

How about a mountain adventure?

Or a space adventure.

A Underground mystery
Indiana Jones, Willy, and Short Round investigate some rumours of 'strange goings on' in the tunnels of a disused Underground tube train station. They have some nasty surprises and Short Round has to get Indiana and Willy out of a sticky situation!

B Shipwreck adventure
Indiana Jones, Willy, and Short Round attempt to search an ancient shipwreck on the ocean floor. Again some nasty surprises await them and they only escape by the skin of their teeth.

What to do next

On your own

1 Use your notes and ideas from the improvisation to write the script for your Indiana Jones adventure.
2 Follow the way the script has been set out on pages 56–59. Remember:
   - each character is named each time they speak
   - stage directions (in brackets) tell where the characters are and how they speak and move
   - ideas for sound and visual effects are also given in stage directions

Heroes and Heroines: Fact or Fiction?

Supergirl

Batman

Tarzan

What to do

In pairs

1 Look at the pictures above. Choose one character and say why you think she or he is a heroine or a hero.
2 Give 3 reasons why your character is like Indiana Jones.
3 Each describe a heroine or hero from a book, play, soap opera, comic or TV drama. Make a list of the things that make this character a heroine or hero.

Real-life heroes and heroines

Princess Anne is a huge help to the Save the Children Fund. She is a tireless worker who gets lots of publicity and helps with all sorts of things. In 1992 we received nearly 100 million pounds. Children would not have benefited from so much aid without her support.

Area Organizer – Preston

Almost everyone agrees that Bob Geldof can be loud and obnoxious and that he constantly uses language that isn't fit for a family newspaper... Yet this man inspires the kind of trust that even the most respected charities can only dream of. People walk up to Geldof with tears in their eyes and stuff wads of money into his hands.

Nathan Aaseng

Doreen Ashburnham, aged 11, and a boy aged 8 were on their way to catch ponies near their home on Vancouver Island. Doreen was attacked by a large mountain lion. The boy drove it off with his fists and pony bridle but was then attacked himself. Doreen got to her feet and fought the mountain lion – she even put her arm into the lion's mouth to try to stop it biting the boy! She got it off him and it fought with her on its back legs before it ran away.

Adapted from *The Register of the George Cross*

What to do

On your own

1 Find out more about one of these real-life heroines or heroes or choose your own. Jot down details about this person, from books, TV, etc., under these 4 headings:
   - Goals or Aims in Life
   - Relationships with Other People
   - Strengths
   - Appearance (if this is important)
2 Complete the following paragraph with 4 or 5 sentences.

   Profile of a real-life heroine/hero

   My idea of a heroine/hero is someone...

END OF UNIT REVIEW

1

2

Oxford University Press, Walton Street, Oxford, OX2 6DP

Oxford New York Toronto
Delhi Bombay Calcutta Madras Karachi
Kuala Lumpur Singapore Hong Kong Tokyo
Nairobi Dar es Salaam Cape Town
Melbourne Auckland Madrid

and associated companies in
Berlin Ibadan

Oxford is a trade mark of Oxford University Press

© Selection and Activities Chris Culshaw and Jill Dodgson 1994
First published by Oxford University Press 1994

ISBN 0 19 831430 2

Cover illustration by Alan Nanson

Printed in Hong Kong

In the same series:

Headwork Book 1	0 19 833372 2
Headwork Book 2	0 19 833373 0
Headwork Book 3	0 19 833374 9
Headwork Book 4	0 19 833375 7
Headwork Book 5	0 19 833387 0
Headwork Book 6	0 19 833388 9
Headwork Book 7	0 19 833389 7
Headwork Book 8	0 19 833390 0
English Headwork Book 1	0 19 833376 5
English Headwork Book 2	0 19 833377 3
English Headwork Book 3	0 19 833378 1
English Headwork Book 4	0 19 833379 X
Headwork Stories Book 1	0 19 833380 3
Headwork Stories Book 2	0 19 833381 1
Headwork Stories Book 3	0 19 833391 9
Headwork Stories Book 4	0 19 833392 7
Headwork Anthologies Book 1	0 19 833396 X
Headwork Anthologies Book 2	0 19 833397 8
Headwork Anthologies Book 3	0 19 833398 6